The Secret Is Out:
It's Time To Break Ground

Lakisha Sanders

authorHOUSE®

AuthorHouse™
1663 Liberty Drive
Bloomington, IN 47403
www.authorhouse.com
Phone: 1-800-839-8640

First published by AuthorHouse   7/26/2010

ISBN: 978-1-4520-3605-2 (e)
ISBN: 978-1-4520-3604-5 (sc)

Library of Congress Control Number: 2010910551

Printed in the United States of America
Bloomington, Indiana

This book is printed on acid-free paper.

Contents

DEDICATED TO RUBY LEE SNELLS

This book is in loving memory to my exceptional, most worthy and well-respected great-grandmother, Ruby Lee Snells. She is the epitome of a strong phenomenal woman. Her life was completely built around her faith. Ruby Lee Snells was indeed compassionate and giving towards others as she opened her doors for various family members to get their start. She was well known for her generous spirit as she fed a plethora of people. She will always be remembered for her kind hearted spirit that was displayed to many.

Although she has gone to be with the Lord, she will never be forgotten. Ruby Lee Snells imparted a wealth of knowledge into my soul. She taught me how to be a real woman and to stand on the Word of God. Over the years, she has served as a mentor who poured bountifully into me being the individual I am today!

Ruby Lee Snells did not have a college degree but she had God and that was enough! She did not allow anyone to separate her from the love of God and she taught her family to do the same. Ruby Lee Snells is the laughter and joy of my heart. She is a tremendous influence in the decisions I make today. Besides being a wonderful inspiration, she was also an extraordinary teacher, amazing singer and an astounding cook!

ACKNOWLEDGEMENTS

Glory, Praise and Honor to the Almighty God for His wondrous works! Without Him, I am nothing! I am forever grateful for the opportunity that God has allowed me to serve as an instrument of His Workmanship to write this book of encouragement to those who may be lost. I would like to thank God most of all for the gift He has instilled in me in order that I may fulfill the anointing through my hands to empower souls everywhere. It is without reservation that I acknowledge my grandmother, Dr. Presiding Elder Emma Mae Lowery. She was someone who did not allow me to give up on anything. She gave me no options on making strides on trying to finish my Doctoral Degree. My Grandmother stood in the gap for me when I could not stand for myself. My loving mother, Reverend Yvonne Johnson who taught me how to overcome the smallest obstacles I tried to make big! She showed me how to pray in order that God would give me a discerning spirit. From then I was able to decipher the difference from the good and evil. My ever caring and gracious Aunt Eylane for all of her hard work! She has taught me to be a woman of strength and courage. I will never find an aunt like Eylane because no one will ever amount to her. My extraordinary Aunt Elizabeth Anthony, one who doesn't mind lending a helping hand to those in need. She is always there to shed light into any given situation. Her powerful words will never be forgotten. My incredible sister, LaShundalin Sanders, I am grateful for you because when I doubted myself, you believed in me. You allowed me to keep going in spite of what others said.

Thank you for allowing me to learn from your situations! My beautiful cousins, Jalethea and Jocelayna Howard! Thank you for your unconditional love and continued support. My handsome nephews, Antoine Jr. and Jermiah Clark! I just thank you for being YOU! My over protective Uncle Ray, you always placed a smile on my face. I am truly grateful for the unseasoned words of wisdom you imparted into my spirit! My Step-Father, Leon Johnson, you told me, "The Sky is the Limit" and I took off! My grandfather, Reverend Joe Louis Lowery, thank you for always finding time to remind me that God is never too busy to fit into my agenda. My favorite cousin, Terence "Terry" Thomas, I love you dearly. Thank you for the inspiring talks that made me stronger! My caring God-Mother, Deaconess Annie Coleman, thank you for the simple yet prominent word you spoke into my life. To Sister Sara Ruth Austin, what a powerful individual! Thank you for speaking life into my situations. A special thank you to the Dania House of God Church and The House of God Churches at Large. To my spiritual father, State Elder Kenny Ellis, I am indeed appreciative of your words of support and encouragement! You brought me through many tough times and I can truly say I am stronger. You are never to busy to speak a word into my spirit. It is my prayer that the Lord forever bless you and keep you! To my mentors, Reverend Chris and Celeste Bolden, I love you all very much! You have added a wealth of inspiration my way and I am truly honored that God has placed you all in my life! To my adoring best friends, Emily Findlater-Webb and Kimberley Billingsley who encouraged me all the way until the end. We have truly formed a bond that is unbreakable. Thank you both for always having my back. Immeasurable gratitude to all of you as reflected in this milestone of accomplishments. Once again, thank you!

Ms. LaKisha Sanders, M.A.Ed, Author

The Secret is Out: It's Time to Break Ground

They said, "You will never amount to anything," I listened. They said, "You will never get accepted into anyone's college," I believed them. They said, "Your dreams are too big," I wanted to give up. They said, She will have two babies before she graduates from college," It kept me up until the wee hours of each morning. They said, "She thinks she all that," It began to make me stronger. In spite of all that I encountered in life, God granted me with His unmerited favor and refused to let me go! The greatest honor is for one to be able to stand in the presence of God. He has placed my feet on a solid foundation that I may be able to withstand the wiles of the devil. God never said the road was going to be easy! However, He has positioned various people in my life to assist with the journey ahead.

Whenever you are awakened by the things of this world, don't think that the enemy is asleep. He is patiently waiting for you to make your first move so he can come in and interrupt God's plan. The devil comes in to seek whom he may devour. He wants to break your character because he knows one can not advance into the kingdom of God without character. It is his desire to harm your careers, your finances and your health. This is not the season to walk in ignorance! Understand, while you are trying to fulfill an assignment and getting things together for this spiritual battle; all hell begins to break loose because the enemy is not pleased. This is the time you need to ask God to open up your spirit and revive the discerning of spirits within you. The enemy knows who you are and who you serve. He assumes the position and tries to place attack on your spirit man in order that you will fall into his trap. The enemy knows that he cannot mess with your character because it is too strong. However, he will attack your weakness and place you around the opposite sex of people that have a form of godliness to test your faith. The Secret is out... your inner man has become exposed. Now, you are in the midst of your home, sleeping with the enemy while enjoying the temptations from the devil himself. He has you right where he wants you... in the palm of his hand. The enemy will come as an angel until he has trapped you in his secret place.

It is vital that you allow the people that God has placed in your life to assist you as you walk towards your destiny. God is trying to develop a greater you and He is looking for you to meet Him half way. God is going to take you to a place that can not be measured with your life. It is going to be impossible to understand how you can be on food stamps and He says, "I am going to give you your own business." It is imperative that you serve as a tool to remind yourself, this earth is not where my feet are going to land but only a pit stop. God is able to do the impossible and make a way out of no way.

This book is designed to empower the lives of those who may be lost and searching for inner peace. It is my prayer that many will become delivered and experience extraordinary self-revelations through a variety of monologues and open-ended questions.

It is my hope that you will realize how God brings people into our lives for numerous reasons, and that often, those people serve as instruments to lighten our heavy loads. We can identify these individuals as "Warning Signs." However, some people feel like throwing in the towel when they hit rocky spots simply because they refuse to be bothered any more. Some feel they are no longer even wanted or needed in this world, and that is when real trouble arises.

If you ever feel you are "not worthy" of anything, you are causing your own destiny to fall into the hands of the enemy. Everything comes full circle in life. For example, some Christians were brought up in the church but wanted to see if the grass was greener on the other side. Yet it is only by the grace of God that all of us are able to come back home. Just because you live in sin does not mean you have to dwell in sin. God gave us His son and His name is Jesus. God said in His word that He came to give us life so that we may have life more abundantly.

"We know that all things work together for good to those who love God, to those who are the called according to His purpose." Romans 8:28 NKJV

Often times, we face circumstances that we are unable to cope with in our lives. This is a scary time to most, but this is also when God comes in to heal, save, set free, and deliver. His word will help transform you and spread light to the person He desires you to be. God has placed various people in your lives to serve as mentors by leading us in the right direction.

If you live according to God's purpose for your life, you will be granted access to your heavenly home. Throughout this journey, you may find that the road ahead is not what you expected. Do not become weary in your well doing because God is going to create a breakthrough as your way of escape. You are a beautiful work in progress, so allow God to transform you into greatness beyond measure. There is no secret to what God can do because He is the source of our present help.

"You Didn't Tell Me"

AIDS Victim: We used to talk every day until you introduced me to this guy. He was the man of my dreams. Tall, fair-skinned, pretty brown eyes...and he had a smile that could send me to Hawaii and back.... He was everything that I could want in a man. It was almost too good to be true. He told me everything. He kept no secrets from me...or at least that's what I thought. YOU... you said, "You really found the right one this time. He's a keeper!" I smiled happily but modestly, because I knew my world would never come to an end with this man.

When I went in for my monthly check-up, the doctor walked back into my room, her face filled with a gravity I had never seen. I asked her, "Doctor, what is wrong? Why do you look like that?" She said, "I'm sorry, Alice, but you are HIV-Positive." Tears began to roll down my face as I continued to stare at the doctor in disbelief. "Doctor, you can't be serious...this was my first encounter...this can not be happening to me." She then asked, "Well, how did you meet him? Did he not warn you of the disease?"

I wondered if you knew He had HIV. I called and inquired and you told me, "Yes, I knew, but I didn't think it was that important. I didn't know you would be another victim..."

A year later, I passed away, thanks to you!

Self-Reflection: Describe an experience with a friend who you thought had good intentions but betrayed you in some way.

_____
_____
_____
_____
_____
_____
_____
_____
_____
_____
_____
_____
_____
_____
_____
_____
_____
_____
_____
_____
_____
_____
_____
_____
_____

Prayer: Dear Lord, help me to seek you first in everything I do. I want to wait patiently on the man/woman that you send to me. In Jesus name I pray, Amen.

"Jesus said, 'The thief does not come except to steal, and to kill, and to destroy. I have come that they may have life, and that they may have it more abundantly.'" John 10:10 NKJV

Jesus has not only promised us life, but life in abundance! In life, you may find yourself worrying about things that are out of your control. But rest assured - every time Satan plans to attack you, God sends angels to watch over you. When "all hell" begins to break loose, remember that you are in a relationship with God, and that He knows all about it. The same God that delivered Job is the same God that will deliver you! When Satan begins attacking your family, ministry, finances, or job, it no longer becomes an ordinary battle but spiritual warfare.

It is impossible to remain in a state of misery and depression and expect God to grant you abundant life. Encourage yourself through prayer and supplication and trust God to do the impossible. Keeping His word close to your heart will bring you contentment in times of uncertainty and give you the abundance of that which matters most. Those who hunger and thirst after the word of God will have what was promised to them in His word.

"You Made Me Drink It"

Alcoholic Victim: I grew up in the streets of New York. I loved being around my family, especially my dad. He taught me everything I knew...how to be a Real Man...how to love... how to overcome my problems by reading my Bible and staying in church.... I always knew that I was rooted and grounded because of what my dad instilled in me from a very early age.

But one night, I heard my dad come home late, fussing at everyone in the house. I knew something was wrong...I heard my mother begin to cry...my younger siblings hid in a corner as they watched my dad beat the living daylights out of my mother - all because he was drunk. After a while, he called me over and said, "Son, come here! I have something for you." I replied, "What is it, Dad?" He said, "Drink some of this, it will teach you how to be a Real Man." I drank the alcohol as fast as I could, just to get it over with. He said, "That's it, Son, drink as much as you can...it will make you feel better." I began to drink up.

From that moment on, I became an alcoholic and began to drink all my problems away. Can you imagine your dad passing you a set of car keys at the age of ten? Well, that's what my dad did to me. My dad told me to get in the car and go for a drive...I guess you can visualize what happened next, right? That's right, another victim... gone...this is how I learned to be a "Real Man" - from a single sip of gin that turned into a pit of HELL!

<u>Self-Reflection</u>: Do you have any family members who may have an addiction to alcohol? How can you help them overcome this fierce battle?

_____
_____
_____
_____
_____
_____
_____
_____
_____
_____
_____
_____
_____
_____
_____
_____
_____
_____
_____
_____
_____
_____
_____

<u>Prayer</u>: Dear Lord, I need you to come through for me right now. I am in dire need of your grace and mercy. Lord, help me to do away with alcohol as I strive to be closer to you. Amen.

"Do not worry about anything, but pray and ask God for everything you need, always giving thanks, and God's peace, which is so great we cannot understand it, will keep your hearts and minds in Christ Jesus."

Philippians 4:6-7 NKJV

When you select peace, you permit God to grant you unmerited favor. It is vital that you practice the life-changing principles that are found in Philippians 4:6-7. Whenever you begin to feel anxiety, you should always pray to conquer worry in your life. Establish a relationship with God and allow Him to steer you to the right path. Prayer is the key that unlocks the door to sovereignty in Christ.

However, prayer is far more than asking God for His assistance; prayer is also a form of worship and thanksgiving. But remember: peace and anxiety cannot co-exist. So if you are going to worry, there is no need to pray. When you do pray, trust and believe that God will do just what He said He would do - take care of you! When you take your burdens to the Lord, leave them there and allow Him to work in your favor. Eliminate unnecessary stress by never allowing worry to invade your worship or praise. God's peace is the best peace man can ever have.

"You Watched Me Die"

Suicidal Victim: "Do your best! We will not settle for anything less than a 'B' from you...."

I was always an honor roll student. I brought home nothing but "A's" and you all were soooo...proud of me. Because you knew that I could do anything, you said to me, "If you bring home anything less than a "B," don't think twice about coming into this house." From that moment on, I knew it was my responsibility to make you all proud. You and Dad were going through hard times and you felt it best if you just got a divorce. I guess you thought that this weight would bypass me somehow - that I wouldn't be affected at all, and that I would continue to be able to focus in school while knowing what was going on.

Needless to say, I saw a big, fat disappointing "C" on my first report card. I remembered your last words to me: "If you bring home anything less than a 'B' don't think twice about coming into this house." I had nowhere to go...I had no one to talk to...I was afraid to go home...especially now that I knew what you and Dad were going through. I guess you thought I didn't see how you dragged Mom across the floor...how you beat her into a pole...I couldn't believe my own eyes.

I pulled out a pocket knife from my purse, which I'd been carrying for protection.... "Someone Please Help Me!!!!" I screamed. People stared in astonishment, but no one came to my rescue. They saw me cut myself with the knife and still no one stopped me. Another cry for help... "Someone Please Help Me!!!!" I began cutting myself until I cut in the wrong place...I guess the people who heard me crying for help thought I would live forever. Sixty seconds later, I was dead. Thanks a lot.

<u>Self-Reflection</u>: How can you assist someone who may be suffering from suicidal thoughts?

_____
_____
_____
_____
_____
_____
_____
_____
_____
_____
_____
_____
_____
_____
_____
_____
_____
_____
_____
_____
_____
_____
_____
_____
_____

<u>Prayer</u>: Dear Lord, I am sorry for the attempt to commit suicide. I ask that you forgive me of all the suicidal thoughts that have entered into my heart. Amen.

"The only temptation that has come to you is that which everyone has. But you can trust God, who will not permit you to be tempted more than you can stand. But when you are tempted, he will also give you a way to escape so that you will be able to stand it."

I Corinthians 10:13 NCV

Everyone faces temptation at some point in his or her life; after all, we are human. But God created an escape route from the enemy through His word. Your escape route may include the power of prayer, fasting, or releasing people out of your life who may have a negative influence on you. The enemy deserves no credit from you. Often, the only reason the enemy is in your presence is that you have given him power. The time to act is now! Leave your own pity party and put the devil back down in his place.

Don't spend a lot of energy focusing on the devil; in fact, give him no attention at all - indifference is the best defense against a spiritual distraction. Continue speaking the Word of God in your life and allow Him to control your every move. Use your God-given abilities to escort enticement out the door of your life. On your worst day, you will be able to knock the devil out with your best shot because you will have the authority. Utilize the tools that God has given you and Praise Him even when you are going through the fire.

"You Abused Me"

Abuse Victim: We were a young couple in high school. I never knew then that my once-simple lifestyle would intertwine with your rough-and-tumble occupation. You were on your way to millionaire status. You turned to me, looked in my eyes, and said, "You can have anything you want...car, house, jewelry...whatever you want, it's yours."

I was certain that I was the happiest woman alive. You gave me my own credit card and told me to feel free to buy whatever I wanted...so I did just that. I came home after shopping, and granted, it was kind of late, but I was home. You greeted me with a slap in the face and told me, "I own you! You belong to me! You will never step back into this house again after 9 p.m.!" I was in shock. I sank down to the floor and said, "I went shopping, just as you said I could." You then sent me to bed and used my body as an instrument. You toiled at me every night – but I was really no longer there; you had bruised my heart and my soul. The abuse and pain I felt was indescribable.

I called YOU and told YOU what was going on, and you replied, "Girl, the man is rich! Do you know how many women he has waiting on him?" I pondered over what you told me and said, "Okay, I will stick it out, just for YOU!" I went out to get pampered at the salon, but when I arrived back home, who knew it would be my last day on earth? That night, after the abuse was over, he killed me! I could have escaped if I had only listened to the small voice above me and inside me. But I didn't, because I wanted the finer things in life so badly.

Self-Reflection: Do you allow the luxurious lifestyles of others dictate your life?

_____
_____
_____
_____
_____
_____
_____
_____
_____
_____
_____
_____
_____
_____
_____
_____
_____
_____
_____
_____
_____
_____
_____
_____
_____

Prayer: Dear Lord, I come to you with thanks for allowing me another opportunity to serve you. I ask that you create a spirit of thankfulness within me so that I will not gravitate to the wiles of the enemy. Amen.

And Jesus said, "For what is a man profited, if he shall gain the whole world, and lose his own soul? Or what shall a man give in exchange for his soul?"

Matthew 16:26 KJV

The path to God is humble and steadfast; it is never loud, boastful, arrogant, or abusive. When you tread on another's body or soul without their consent, you darken your own soul. God wants us to be happy and have the fine things that He has left for us in this world, but never at the expense of losing our souls or, worse, trading them to the devil.

Our dear Father wants us to meet Him halfway; we must remember to always pray for what we believe God wants of us, and not what we think we want - and we must also work and do our part to show Him that we are grateful for His heavenly assistance. Remember this, and the temple of your soul will always be at rest with the Lord; He will never, ever leave you when you shine your light toward Him alone.

"You Let Me Fall"

Nervous Breakdown Victim: Okay...okay...I'm losing my tenacity. I almost thought I'd lost the one thing I'm most sane with... my mind! Oh, so you think I'm hilarious? You are the reason that I have these nervous breakdowns. I bet you don't know what happens next, do you? Well, I'm longing my mom's oxtails with collard greens, macaroni & cheese, fried cornbread with hot sweet potato pie, OMG! But...guess what? It's gone! How is it that I can place a plate on the counter, and when I come back for it, it's gone? How is that? Did a plate full of my favorite things just walk right out of the kitchen? Who got me for my plate? This is clearly not happening. I'm going crazy. I'm fussing with everyone. Do I look stupid? Do you know who you're dealing with? What an atrocious offense. Everyone is affected by this Nervous Breakdown. Get this - I went to Home Depot to calm my nerves, and can you imagine what the salesman said to me? You can't, can you? You don't know what it's like! He said, "Sir, you may need to find another store because we don't serve your kind here.." Well, then I was really ready to lose my mind. I spotted a ladder, and fueled with my anxiety, I climbed the ladder and I screamed at the top of my lungs, "Can someone save me!" Everyone just stood there, looking at me in amazement. I screamed again, "Can someone save me?" Do you know what happened next? I fell off that 32-foot ladder and died on the scene.

Self-Reflection: How can you prevent anxiety from occuring in your life?

_____
_____
_____
_____
_____
_____
_____
_____
_____
_____
_____
_____
_____
_____
_____
_____
_____
_____
_____
_____
_____
_____
_____
_____
_____
_____

Prayer: Dear Lord, I am suffering from anxiety and need your guidance. Allow me to take things one day at a time. Help me to trust in you at all times, Amen.

"The Lord is my strength and my shield; my heart trusted in Him, and I am helped; therefore my heart greatly rejoiceth; and with my song will I praise Him."
Psalm 28:7 KJV

It is no secret that God is always within you and all around you - though you may sometimes feel the world is too much for you, and your anxiety and depression is insurmountable, just look to the Lord for guidance, and He will be glad to take your burdens from you and let you heal.

However, you must be prepared to let Him heal you; let Him take over the reins of control when you feel you can't carry the weight of anxiety or depression any longer. You are responsible for voluntarily and submissively handing over your troubles to God - through prayer and faith, He will work wonders in your life, but you must allow Him entrance.

"You Let Me Go"

Runaway Child: To all who looked in from the outside perspective, it was such a pretty picture. Friends and family, even, thought we were the perfect family and had the ideal relationship with one another. I did everything right - or at least that's what I thought. I sang praises to God and worshipped God and even spoke sometimes at Sunday services. I never did any wrong to anyone.

But instead of speaking life into me, you spoke of death. I wondered why you had so many negative things to say about your own child. You told me that I would never amount to anything. You said no one would ever love me. You even told me that you would run me over with your own truck and turn yourself in...how can you be so evil to your own child? Yet with the same mouth, you say, "I love you!"

I'm confused...now no one in my family wants me...you spoke to all of our family and told them to disown me. You kicked me out of your house and told me to never come back. I listened...and now you've labeled me a "runaway child" with nowhere to go, and you don't even care. The price tag is on my shirtsleeve...I was sold to a family who believed in molesting children and cutting them up into small pieces and burning them! Another one, gone! You wanted a perfect family? Well, you got it - without me!

<u>*Self-Reflection*</u>: *Have you ever felt left out or alone? How did you go about handling being alone/left out?*

_____
_____
_____
_____
_____
_____
_____
_____
_____
_____
_____
_____
_____
_____
_____
_____
_____
_____
_____
_____
_____
_____
_____
_____
_____
_____
_____

<u>*Prayer*</u>: *Dear Lord, I am your child, and I feel all alone. Please allow me to be confident in myself. Please love me. Amen.*

"A new commandment that I give unto you; That ye love one another; as I have loved you, that ye also love one another. By this shall all men know that ye are my disciples, that ye also love one another."

John 14: 34-35 KJV

It is a sad truth that so many in this great world of ours, with so many people, feel very alone. I'm sure you've all heard the adage, "One can feel loneliest in a crowd" and other, similar sayings that shed light on this deeply sorrowful emotion. Now, think about it: If God intended for us to be alone, He would have made just one of us - but He didn't! He created Adam and Eve so that they would respect, love, and communicate with each other.

The world is not a lonely place unless you make it so; there are always "strangers who are friends you haven't met" around every corner - if you just look. But even during the dark night of the soul - that still, quiet time when the only sound you can seem to hear is your own breath, always know that you are never alone - God is always within you and near you, and He promised you and all of us here on earth that he would never leave. Now that's something! You can count on God, and you can pray to Him to relieve you of your loneliness. But in the meantime, know that He is there.

"You Set Me Up"

Gang Violence Victim: Who are you to tell me no? What gives you the right to give me advice? I know who you really are beneath all of your fancy suits and seventy-dollar hairstyles. I don't need to listen; you never listened to me...I was a little girl searching for a mother who would hold me with all her might. You lost yourself when my father died; you might as well say you lost me too. You always said I could depend on family - yeah, right, family - what's that, anyway? Guess what? I don't remember any more!

I was lonely, miserable, and wanted nothing more but you! You left me to fend for myself so one day I didn't have to fend for myself any more. They welcomed me in...something you never did. I finally found what was missing - all they asked for was my loyalty. That's it! They were just like me - they had someone in their lives just like you - giving them advice that they were not following themselves.

No one understood our bond - not our parents and definitely not the cops. To them we were riffraff; abandoned regrets that no one wanted. They were mine, and no one was going to take them away from me - not you, and certainly not the cops.

As part of initiation, I was expected to leave you, my birth family, and join their family. We were dared! So I gave my family the loyalty they asked from me...all the way down to the last bullet, which landed directly in my heart.

I lived for you to love me and I died for loving them too much.

Self-Reflection: Have you been tempted to do something that you knew was wrong? How did you determine whether or not to get involved? Did you resist the temptation or not?

_____
_____
_____
_____
_____
_____
_____
_____
_____
_____
_____
_____
_____
_____
_____
_____
_____
_____
_____
_____
_____
_____
_____
_____

Prayer: Dear Lord, I am submitting myself wholeheartedly to you. Please help me to stay away from temptation. Amen.

*"The way of the wicked is an abomination unto the Lord;
nut He loveth him that followeth unto righteousness.
Correction is grievous unto him that forsaketh the way,
and he that hateth reproof shall die."*

Proverbs 15: 9-10 KJV

When you truly know that God is with you, a very unusual but delightful thing happens: You begin to realize that you lose the desire to sin against Him; you will gradually begin to question your own actions before taking the next step forward – or backward.

This happens because when you accept God into your heart, all things come to you from God, including His infinite wisdom, peace, and love that he places on you and inside you, wherever you go. And with that holy balm of His spirit over your head, you will not feel the need to commit a sin, trespass against the Lord's words in any way, or fall down to temptation or its companions. When you have God's heart in your own heart, you walk together as one, and life is easier when "two are more are gathered" in His name, as our Lord said.

God is always with you, and He always sees what you do. Make sure whatever you do is what will be most pleasing to Him, and you will feel comforted and guided!

"Lost In The Fire"

Reprobated Mind Victim: It was hard for me growing up, even since childhood. Everyone had big dreams for me.... yeah... especially you. I even saw myself changing for a moment and then you begin nagging me and speaking negatively about me until I felt the change was unimportant. Sometimes you'd say, "Although you're going through a tough time, everything is going to be alright." There was a time when giving up was not an option. You said to me, "Excellence is your Purpose. Failing will never be considered. Always strive to be the best because giving up will never be an option in this house."

It was obvious that you were going through your own problems...it was obvious that you needed someone to turn to...but I felt as though you left me hanging...man...after a while, I began to do my own thing. I forgot about the church! I forgot about all the morals that I had been taught as a child. I let myself go.

Once you seemed to be back to your "normal self," and you wanted to talk to me about life and positive living and get me back on the right track...but I have to laugh, because it's pitiful...it was too late!

I finally went back to church. The preacher tried to pray for me... huh.... Can you fathom that his prayer did nothing for me? My mind was completely gone. The preacher looked at you and said, "If prayer can't fix it, neither can I."

I needed you...I needed you...I needed you! I lost everything...I thought I knew it all. People tried to come to my rescue, but by that time, I was stuck in my own ways.

I saw you at Highland Park...you saw me sitting alone, but you didn't bother to say two words...a stray bullet hit me right in my heart...I reached out to you and you looked at me and said, "You needed a wake-up call.... Say good-bye!" I died that night with you standing over my body.

Self-Reflection: Was there ever a time when you wanted to give up on life? Have you ever felt you were losing your mind? How did you get back on the right track?

_____
_____
_____
_____
_____
_____
_____
_____
_____
_____
_____
_____
_____
_____
_____
_____
_____
_____
_____
_____
_____
_____
_____
_____
_____
_____

Prayer: Dear Lord, help me stay focused on you and not give into diverse, earthly temptations. I want more of you in my life because I refuse to go astray. Amen.

"And he said unto his disciples, 'Therefore I say unto you, take no thought for your life; what ye shall eat; neither for the body, what ye shall put on. The life is more than meat, and the body is more than raiment.'"
Luke 12: 22-23 KJV

Before you were born, God instilled wisdom within you that is uniquely your own; without this, you would be just like everyone else, and you would need to follow others to know where to go. But because God has given you the gift of a clean, individual mind, He expects you to use this gift to the best of your ability and never get so sidetracked or distracted with others' lifestyles, ideas, or words, that you abandon your own. Your body is your temple, God said, and your mind is what holds that temple secure.

Do not disappoint our Lord any more than you have to by going against your own intuition, your own inner vision, and your own thoughts and words – because He gave them to you as His personal blessing, upon your birth. You have a strong mind; use it well!

"She Didn't Reject Me"

Homosexual Spirit Victim: You cut my hair because you said, "You'll look better this way." I was still young, so I no say in the matter...you had no idea what I experienced at school. Girls were trying me...boys were trying me...even the faculty and staff were trying me...

You had no clue how and what I felt with the new "me" you were creating. Every day, I passed a mirror and asked to myself, "Am I a boy or a girl?" I was confused! I couldn't get a date. I got rejected each time I asked a boy out. I tried to come home and fill you in on what was happening to me, and you were too tired to listen.

One day the time had come for me to try something new. Since I was getting rejected by all the boys, I wanted to know if I would get the same rejection from the girls. Well, let's just say I didn't get rejected...yeah, someone accepted me for me...I came home and although you were tired, you took another look at me and said, "Gina, what have you done?" I replied, "I tried to talk to you. I tried to fill you in on what was going on, but you didn't have time to fit me into your schedule."

You stared at me for a moment and said, "Gina, I command you right now to go upstairs and change your attire at once." I shook my head and said, "It's too late now; the damage is already done." You looked up to heaven and said, "I'm sorry, Lord, but if I can't have my own child back, then no one can." You shot me twice in the back and then shot yourself.

<u>Self-Reflection</u>: What are some things you can do to assist a friend or family member who you know is considering homosexuality?

_____
_____
_____
_____
_____
_____
_____
_____
_____
_____
_____
_____
_____
_____
_____
_____
_____
_____
_____
_____
_____
_____
_____
_____
_____
_____
_____
_____

<u>Prayer</u>: Dear Lord, I know you created Adam and Eve, not Adam and Steve. I also know that the very thought of being a homosexual is an abomination unto you. Lord, help me as I strive to be more like you. Amen.

"I am the vine: ye are the branches. He that abideth in me, and I in him, the same bringeth forth much fruit: for without me, ye can do nothing. If a man abide not in me, he is cast forth as a branch, and is withered; and men gather them, and cast them into the fire, and they are burned. If ye abide in me, and my words abide in you, ye shall ask what ye will, and it will be done unto you." John 15: 5-7 KJV

God's love for us is so much larger and greater than we could ever imagine in our mere human's eyes. Love that great, should always be treated with the utmost respect and returned with the nobility which it was given. Whenever you feel in doubt regarding your personal behavior, just look to God and ask Him and pray about your situation, and He and His angels will come near you, place His hands on your head, and stay beside you to ensure you do the things He intended just for you in this life. Never worry; to worry or to fear is to acknowledge the absence of God.

"You Never Cared"

High School Dropout Victim: You served as my mentor for a few years, and it was a nice feeling. You took me to school and picked me up because of my mom's busy schedule. As a family, we really didn't have much, but we made do... The children at school always picked on me for numerous reasons. Sometimes, you sat there and laughed right along with them. I didn't understand...I thought you were someone I could depend on for anything...I was in a state of depression...I felt all alone...

After this, I had no one to turn to. The next morning came and you continuously blew the horn for me to come out...you didn't bother to come inside and see if there were a problem or not. You drove back home in your nice BMW. I made a decision to call it quits with high school. No one else cared, so why should I? I became just another person.

I didn't care any more...I started hanging out on street corners and doing my own thing. I remember Thursday morning - I was standing at the corner store and you drove right past me...I looked at you and shook my head. It was like you gave up on me...yet you called yourself my mentor?

All of a sudden, a strange car drove by with tinted windows and gunshots began to fly everywhere. I was in the wrong spot at the wrong time. I died from a stray bullet.

_____

_____

_____

_____

_____

_____

_____

_____

_____

_____

_____

_____

_____

_____

_____

_____

_____

_____

_____

_____

_____

_____

_____

_____

_____

Prayer: _Dear Lord, keep me on the right track so that I will be motivated to continue high school. I can't make it without you, Lord, so please keep me in your care. Amen._

"And he cometh unto the disciples, and findeth them asleep, and saith unto Peter, 'What, could ye not watch with me one hour? Watch and pray, that ye enter not into temptation; the spirit indeed is willing, but the flesh is weak.'" Matthew 26: 40-41 KJV

It is always a good thing to have teachers and mentors in your life, whatever your age, for learning never stops. But when you begin to lean too much on the other person to continue your own efforts, you are holding yourself back and giving up on your own potential within. God set you apart; He made certain that he set you up with many individuals with whom you will come into contact to help and guide you – and he also put your foes in front of you to see whether you would be able to recognize them in His sight.

Do not let down the Lord when it comes to your own self-confidence and strength from within – He is counting on you to spread the goodness, peace, and love that can only come from Him, and without knowledge and proper education, academic and otherwise, who will listen to you? Be a good steward of Christ and continue to advance your mind, and God will treasure you forever for this. Remember: learning never stops for those who are truly wise!

"You Watched Me Suffer"

Spirit of Grief Victim: It's morning…the funeral is over. I can't believe it; Dad's gone. He was just here yesterday, in good health. Why me, Lord? He was my best friend. My dad was my everything.

After the service, I was a bit distraught to see you, my own mother acting as though nothing had even happened. I was worried for a minute because I knew that you and Dad had the perfect marriage…at least that's the picture you painted for your children.

It really vexed my spirit when I saw you starting to get all glamorous to go out - every night! Monday, Tuesday, Wednesday, Thursday, Friday, Saturday, and even Sundays. How in the name of common sense could you do this to yourself? How could you do this to your children? Not once did you ask us if we were hurting. Not once did you ask us if we were suffering in school from the spirit of grief.

For crying out loud, when we tried to talk to you, you walked right past us as if we did not even exist. My siblings and I were frustrated. Not only did we lose our father, but we were losing our mother, too. I tried to remain strong for my brothers and sisters, but I couldn't do it any longer because I was hurting…I felt helpless…I'm crying out for help.…

I'm grieving, and I needed you…you were not the only person hurting. Your children were hurting. Remember us?

I went for a walk to calm my nerves. Somehow, I ended up on one of the highest bridges I had ever seen. I thought about what was going on in my life, and I was still miserable and confused. I looked down at all the random people walking, at all the stores and ongoing traffic under me...then I looked up to heaven and said, "Dad, I'm coming to be with you because I know you will listen to me."

I closed my eyes and landed on heaven's doorstep. Prayerfully, God will let me in...because I believe He will listen.

Self-Reflection: How do you deal with a loss of a close relative or friend?

_____

_____

_____

_____

_____

_____

_____

_____

_____

_____

_____

_____

_____

_____

_____

_____

_____

_____

_____

_____

_____

_____

_____

_____

Prayer: Dear Lord, help me find comfort in your infallible word so that I may be a shinning light unto others. In Jesus name I pray, Amen.

Come unto me, all that labor and are heavy laden, and I will give you rest. Take my yoke, and learn of me; for I am meek and lowly in heart; and ye shall find rest unto your souls. For my yoke is easy, and my burden is light."
Matthew 12: 28-30 KJV

Sorrow and grief are very real feelings, and sadly, they are part of the life that God gave us. But before God takes anything away, He gives us the love of it so that we may always cherish and remember that personal gift. Just as when someone you love passes away into God's Kingdom, you have lost the body and the presence of your loved one, but in spirit, love never dies.

Turn to God with all of your troubles and in all of your grief; there is no grief that is too great to hand over to the Lord - He is all-powerful and will take on your burdens when they become too heavy for you to carry. But you must call on God; let Him know you need Him, and he will come. The grief you feel means that you have exchanged love with another person, and love, as God said, is the greatest gift of all.

"You Forgot About Us"

Homeless Spirit Victim: It wasn't easy for me...my dad left when I was 7 years old...he didn't have a care in the world because he was wealthy. My mom had four other children besides me to take care of, and I was left to tend to them while she worked two jobs just to make ends meet.

My mother attempted to contact my father to see if he would be willing to lend a helping hand, especially because he had left his five children with no father. He replied, "Both you and those kids are no longer my responsibility. I have my own family to take care of now."

Wow! Really? It's funny...I think back to how we moved from apartment to apartment, six people sharing one room, creating makeshift beds out of sheets, sniggling together to keep warm during the winter season, while you, Dad, slept in your plush, king-size bed, lying next to the woman you had an affair with. And your "own family" you had to "take care of" were all lying peacefully in their own, private rooms.

At 7 a.m. on February 1, an eviction notice was nailed to our door. I had no other choice but to join the other men and women who stood in the middle of the street holding signs saying, "Will Work for Food."

The sad thing is, I really was willing to work...I just needed to eat...but I was hit by a drunk driver and died instantly. Thank you, Dad!

Self-Reflection: How do you respond to the homeless you pass on the street? What can you do to improve the quality of their lives?

_____
_____
_____
_____
_____
_____
_____
_____
_____
_____
_____
_____
_____
_____
_____
_____
_____
_____
_____
_____
_____
_____
_____
_____
_____
_____
_____
_____
_____
_____

Prayer: Dear Lord, bless those who are homeless or on the verge of losing their homes. Grant them the serenity that only you can, despite the circumstances they face. In Jesus' name, Amen.

"I will greatly rejoice in the Lord, my soul shall be joyful in my God; for he hath clothed me with the garments of salvation, he hath covered me with the robe of righteousness, as a bridegroom decketh himself with ornaments, and as a bride adorneth herself with her jewels." Isaiah 61:10 KJV

There comes a time in everyone's life when he or she feels like "running away." It's true; none of us are exempt from that natural urge to free ourselves and be independent of those whom we perceive as our "jailors," when, in essence, they are our true companions. As they say, "The grass is always greener on the other side" - or so it would seem; the truth is, it is not greener, more beautiful, easier, or better. God puts us where we are supposed to be and gives us the tools to use in those places.

Nothing is by "accident" under God's great plan; trust in your process, and know that everything you do and everywhere you go and everyone you meet are in some way meant to help you become a better person for God and for your family. To leave what seems "not good enough" is to give up, plain and simple. God frowns on those who dismiss His grand plans - do you want to be among those?

"You Starved Me"

Eating Disorder Victim: I'm really not certain how this happened. Wait...it was you...yeah, my own mother! How could I forget? One night, Dad brought home a box of Kentucky Fried Chicken and you sent me straight to my room. I was so hungry! I was furious!

I knew you felt frustrated because you wanted me to be on your magazine cover...you kept saying that all I needed to do was lose 20 more pounds to be in your Top 10 for the next Teenzine magazine. I was already 90 pounds dripping wet... who ever knew you were out to get your own daughter?

As we all sat in the family room watching television, you sent me to bed early. I overheard you and Dad talking, and you told him, "I don't think she will cut it for this magazine cover. Although she's our daughter, she's not as fit as all the other girls."

Those words that will be forever embedded in my mind... do you know how much that haunts me? I always wanted to please you, but your actions showed me that you really didn't care. So, I decided to stop eating because I figured it would make you feel better about your own child. I began sticking my index finger down my throat as far as I could. I did it every night until instead of vomiting, my own stomach acid came up my throat and out through my nose and immediately in your face! I didn't mean to...or did I? My body was a statue of skeleton bones...you saw what was happening and did nothing.

Three weeks later, I died in your kitchen, waiting on my plate from two months ago! Am I skinny enough for you now?

Self-Reflection: Do you know someone who suffers from an eating disorder? How can you assist them in overcoming this disease?

_____
_____
_____
_____
_____
_____
_____
_____
_____
_____
_____
_____
_____
_____
_____
_____
_____
_____
_____
_____
_____
_____
_____
_____
_____

Prayer: Dear Lord, open my eyes so that I may see when I begin to go down the wrong path. Give me the sense of urgency to value my health so that I may fulfill the plan you have for me. In Jesus' name, Amen.

"Behold the fig tree, and all the trees; when they now shoot forth, ye see and know of your own selves that summer is now nigh at hand...And take heed to yourselves, lest at any time your hearts be overcharged with surfeiting, and drunkenness, and cares of this life, and so that day come upon you unawares."

Luke 21: 29-31; 34-35 KJV

You are always the best judge of yourself. Your body is your temple, as God has made it so, and you must not mistreat or deny or abuse this beautiful vehicle so lovingly made by the hands of our Lord. Others' perceptions of you do not have any bearing on your life; what others say and think about how you look, speak, or wear your clothes has nothing whatsoever to do with who you are - a Holy child of Christ.

   If you ever feel pressured or tempted to "go with the ways of the masses," just pray to God to keep true to yourself, and He will provide an answer. There is no goodness where God is absent, and there is never happiness or fulfillment where there is self-denial and conformity to others' beliefs and values. Listen to your own heart and your own mind; it is there for a reason!

"I Reached a New High"

Crack head Victim: We had been dating for five years...we were hanging out in your apartment...alone...and one night, I felt you twitch nervously in your sleep.

In a loud voice you screamed, "I can't take it!" At that moment, I was truly perplexed. I looked over at you as you pulled out a tan pouch from your book bag and poured it on the coffee table. I sat in horror as I saw needles, a straw, and white bags of cocaine.

You turned to me and suggested that I try it because it would make me feel better. I trusted you...so I did it! It's too bad I did not know then that this was the beginning of the roughest journey of my life.

I went from weekend shots to skipping school. When even that became too much, school was no longer my priority and dropping out was my only option. My mother put her foot down and refused to let me use at home, so the crack house became my new home. The more chaos that existed in my life, the higher I tried to get.

Do you realize that you ruined me? Do you realize that you completely destroyed my life??? I'm worthless... nothing...this..."feel-good medicine"...this white powder... it's everything to me now...it means the world to me...you used to mean the world to me, but now.... It's my goal to get as much and as high as I can. So that's what I did! I got very, very high...until I felt a new type of high... one called death.

Self-Reflection: Do you know someone addicted to drugs? Have you neglected their cries for help? What can you do now to help them break their addiction?

_____
_____
_____
_____
_____
_____
_____
_____
_____
_____
_____
_____
_____
_____
_____
_____
_____
_____
_____
_____
_____
_____
_____
_____
_____
_____
_____

Prayer: Dear Lord, forgive me for failing to withstand temptation. Cleanse me of all impurities. Let this be my testimony so I may help someone else. In Jesus' name, Amen.

"And Jesus said unto him, 'No man, having put his hand to the plough, and looking back, is fit for the kingdom of God." Luke 9:62 KJV

It seems that everywhere we look these days, we are confronted with all kinds of temptation in the form of substances that can coerce and fool us into thinking that we have found "heaven on earth." There is no drug, no amount of alcohol, food, sex, gambling, or other distraction that is as pure and good and full as that which waits for you in God's kingdom.

Do you think you have to wait for your soul to go to heaven to find this sense of wholeness and serenity? If so, you are mistaken; the goods of the Lord are well within your reach - simply put your hand out, with your eyes closed in prayer, and ask God to deliver you to the purity of His kingdom here on earth.

The finest things in life are easy to obtain, full of abundance, and non-restrictive. Don't let drugs or other alternative substances or diversions capture your attention when you can bask in the peacefulness of the Lord every day, for free!

"Morning Never Came"

Prostitute Spirit Victim: Do you think I'm still beautiful? For the mere 17 years of my life, I never felt pretty. I remember once you tried to place me in some kind of frilly little thing, covered with tiny pink flowers. It made me look like a potted plant...ridiculous...like a clown...yet I looked to you as my role model. You were the epitome of what a strong, black Christian woman should be. I admired your confidence because it was something I didn't have...confidence was so difficult for me because of my appearance.

One day after church, you said you were going to take me to your place of employment. I was really excited because I wanted so much to emulate a woman of such status and greatness. As we neared your "office," I saw strange women dressed up in such sleazy attire, I leaned over to ask you, "What in heaven's name is going on here?" You replied, "No need to worry, honey; this is what I do."

I knew then that my mind was gone.... You said to me, "Your outfit is in the back...you are going to be rich tonight." I thought about it...I sure needed the money to help my mom out since Dad was no longer a part of our household, so I started to put on the filmy, gaudy garment. I said, "If this is how I can obtain greatness, then give it to me...all of it!

You sat back and watched me as I made a fool of myself. You said, "I'm going to leave you now; there are plenty of people to protect you. I will see you in the morning. But morning never came for me....

_____
_____
_____
_____
_____
_____
_____
_____
_____
_____
_____
_____
_____
_____
_____
_____
_____
_____
_____
_____
_____
_____
_____
_____
_____
_____
_____

Prayer: Dear Lord, forgive me for defiling your temple. I realize that disrespecting my body is equivalent to disrespecting you. Thank you for deliverance. Amen.

"But those things that proceed out of the mouth come forth from the heart; and they defile the man. For out of the heart proceed evil thought, murders, adulteries, fornications, thefts, false witness, blasphemies; These are the things which defile a man."

Matthew 16: 18-20 KJV

God so loved us that he created a pure place for our soul to rest while it passes time on earth. That pure place is our vehicle, our body, which we use every day and much too often take for granted. Do you realize that everywhere our spirit goes, our body goes, as well?

Don't trick yourself into thinking that, "I'm really not doing this deed; my mind isn't engaged or interested in it - only my body, so it doesn't count." That is the easy, lazy way out! Your body houses your soul, which was given to you without sin and blessed by God with all of His might and strength. When you soil your body through devious or filthy circumstances, you also leave your spirit unclean, and an unclean spirit is never welcome in the House of the Lord.

"I Kept it in the Family"

Child Molestation Victim: She wanted it...so I took what was mine. I took her young flesh as though it belonged to me. I took from her what my stepfather took from me at the tender age of six. It didn't matter how loud I screamed. It didn't matter that I was a boy. I was alone...and afraid. I was his...slave.

So, my plans were to make this girl mine. I didn't care how much she cried. I didn't care that I was hurting her. It didn't even matter that she was my little sister. Yet, as I looked into her eyes...I saw a part of myself, or at least who I used to be.

Then I realized that I was still the same little boy who cried, pleaded, and begged for a savior. I hated you with every fiber of my being; with all the fury and rage that crawled under my skin. I hate myself today for becoming you...I can no longer hurt anyone because you came home and saw me on top of your little girl. You tore the flesh from my broken bones. Ironically, for one moment...one split second...I was grateful...for you.

<u>Self-Reflection</u>: Were you molested as a child? How has it affected you? How can you help someone else who has suffered the same thing?

_____
_____
_____
_____
_____
_____
_____
_____
_____
_____
_____
_____
_____
_____
_____
_____
_____
_____
_____
_____
_____
_____
_____
_____
_____
_____
_____
_____

<u>Prayer</u>: Dear Lord, forgive the person who took my innocence. Cleanse my mind so that I don't make the same mistakes. Thank you for the people you will take me to, to help them receive their deliverance. In Jesus' name, Amen.

"And if any obey not our word by this epistle, note that man, and have no company with him, that he may be ashamed. Yet count him not as an enemy, but admonish him as a brother."

II Thessalonians 3: 14-15 KJV

It is only through forgiveness that we attain true freedom. It is also arguably one of the hardest things to do – forgive the one person or several persons who harmed you to such an extent that it has haunted you as long as you can remember. But it is blessed to forgive! God will smile upon you and shine a new light on your face when you pray in all earnestness to forgive your enemies or those who may have made your life a living hell. Remember: to forgive is divine!

"Lies Do Hurt"

Lying Spirit Victim: We were always taught to tell the whole truth and nothing but the truth. On our way home from Disney World, we made a pit stop and everyone got out of the car. We turned toward the shopping malls, but Daddy strayed toward the local bar.

An hour later, Daddy reappeared, and Mom said, "Honey, where were you?" He replied, "Sweetie, I went into the Men's Warehouse, you know that's my favorite store. Besides, I needed a few new suits."

I quietly slid over to my dad and said, "Daddy, I saw you go into that bar." Softly, he responded, "Baby, it's just a little white lie; it won't hurt anybody."

From that moment, I felt that nothing was really wrong with lying. I started lying about eating candy before dinner, about doing my homework, about breaking Mom's China, and about taking money from Daddy's wallet. It seemed fun, in a way - I almost felt like, "Hey, what can I come up with today?"

Well, one day I lied to the wrong people. A few fellow liars of mine robbed the local Federal bank. The FBI questioned me concerning my whereabouts and whether or not I knew anything. Without thinking, I denied it all, even though the robbers had told me their complete plans the day before.

Guess what? My "little lies" didn't work for me any more. I was found guilty and given ten to twenty years in prison. It seems like a little white lie does hurt, after all.

Self-Reflection: Have you ever lied for no reason? What prompted you to begin lying? What can you do to change your lying ways?

_____
_____
_____
_____
_____
_____
_____
_____
_____
_____
_____
_____
_____
_____
_____
_____
_____
_____
_____
_____
_____
_____
_____
_____
_____
_____

Prayer: Dear Lord, forgive me; I know that lying is not of you. Help me to be truthful to myself so that I can be truthful to others. In Jesus' name, Amen.

"Holding fast the faithful word as he hath been taught, that he may be able by sound doctrine both to exhort and to convince the gainsayers. For there are many unruly and vain talkers and deceivers."

The Epistle of Paul to Titus 1: 9-11 KJV

Because we are human, we do have faults, and we will also succumb to those faults from time to time. However, God made us in His image for a reason - so that we may follow in His footsteps and live by His example and never be without the sense of glory and peace that He bestowed upon us at our birth.

Lying is one of the most grievous sins, and it is never worth it - because God knows everything that you think, do, say, and perform in life. You may think that you are deceiving God, or that you can simply confess your sins and repent and be forgiven, but it isn't a "formula" and should never be treated as one.

When we lie, even to ourselves, we are discrediting God and doing a harsh disservice to ourselves and those who love us. The truth is beautiful; set it free within you!

"Wrong Delivery"

Drug Dealer Victim: You always reminded me that hanging out on the corner was the wrong thing to do. My mom trusted you with me...her only son. You promised her that you would make sure that I stayed on the straight and narrow path. I looked up to you especially, because I had no brothers or sisters.

When you were invited to a formal social with your fraternity brothers, I was really excited. Men of Strength... Men of Honor...Men of Intellect.

I asked you, "How can I be down?" You laughed, and I thought to myself, "Why is this question so funny?" You looked at me and said, "It takes hard work and long hours," so I replied, "That's fine; just tell me what I need to do."

You gave me a bag and told me to take it to the gentleman standing over in the corner. You also instructed me to wait there until he gave me a package. I wanted to be that Man of Strength, that Man of Honor, that Man of Intellect.

I was going on two years strong. I wanted to be just like you...I established my own clientele...I was slowly making my way to the top. I became the best at delivering poison to my community.

One week later, I made the wrong delivery...to an undercover cop. He had no mercy! The judge gave me a life sentence. Now my "life" is over.

Self-Reflection: Do you know someone who sells drugs? What have you done to help them leave that way of living?

_____
_____
_____
_____
_____
_____
_____
_____
_____
_____
_____
_____
_____
_____
_____
_____
_____
_____
_____
_____
_____
_____
_____
_____
_____

Prayer: Dear Lord, I realize that selling drugs is of the devil and does not line up with your plan for my life. Help me to leave that lifestyle in my past and walk in your will. In Jesus' name, Amen.

"The Lord knoweth how to deliver the godly out of temptations, and to reserve the unjust unto the day of judgement to be punished."

2 Peter 2:9 KJV

Whenever you feel instinctively that something you're doing is not quite "right," then you'd better listen - because God gave you those instincts as an inner compass to show you right from wrong - especially when it isn't evident. If you ever feel you're caught up in the wrong crowd or starting to change too much to the point at which you don't even really like or recognize yourself, how will God recognize you?

It is very easy to fall into the greedy grasp of the devil because the devil works very insidiously; it's a subtle process, but one day, you wake up and think, "How did I get here? Who am I?" Don't wait until that day - listen to your God-given instincts early on in the game so you'll have time to get out before it's too late.

The last thing you want to do is become easy prey for the devil, but you must stand fast and watchful of your soul at all times because though God works in mysterious ways, the devil works through subtle manipulation.

Be ever-watchful and vigilant of your activities - the purity of your soul depends on it!

"Instant Gratification"

Rape Victim: You were my only friend...my only brother...and the only one I could talk to. You said, "Hey, you can come to me about anything!" I loved being around you because you were my hero. You often allowed me to tag along with you and your friends as you played basketball or video games and even went to church on some occasions.

I was really excited because your friends became brothers to me, too, and they didn't allow anyone to even think about bothering me. I felt so loved! So protected!

One weekend, you invited me to a social gathering with you and your friends. It was a great chance for me to hang out with my one and only brother...and all of my new "brothers," as well! I was psyched!

But when I arrived at the gathering, I saw your friends standing there, eyeing me down. I almost felt like they saw me as a piece of meat and instantly became hungry! I became uncomfortable because this was new to me...I was not used to this behavior from them.

I asked you take me home because I knew something wasn't right. But you insisted that I stay...I told you I was uncomfortable...you glared at me and said, "Look, if I have to tell you 'no' one more time, I am going to toss your body in that nice little river across the street."

I never heard you speak to me in that manner...I sat in a corner, all alone, just waiting for the night to end... but to my surprise, it was only the beginning! You told me to go upstairs because you said it would be a long night.

So, because I trusted you, I did! I thought I would be safe there, especially with your friends downstairs.

Suddenly, I began hearing strange noises...then knocks at the door..."Wait a minute," I thought..."These guys are busting through my room like a pack of wolves looking for their prey!" It was very dark; I couldn't see anyone...they began ripping the clothes off my body and viciously throwing me against the headboard. I was screaming at the top of my lungs..."Please STOP! Don't do this to me!" It was my first time...I was a virgin...I couldn't take the pain!

Through the darkness and the unfamiliar setting, faces started to become clear, and yours instantly stood out to me. I couldn't believe it! How could you? My only brother..."The Hero."

The betrayal, the lies, the deceit...every ounce of restraint meant nothing as the fight in me slowly died. It didn't bother you that I was your sister. You and your friends wanted it and made me your slave! You sat there and watched all fifteen of your friends pulverize my body and macerate it like a piece of meat!

I was forced to board the midnight train of horror that led to a death like none other! Thanks a lot!

<u>Self-Reflection</u>: Have you ever been raped or know someone who has been? How did you cope? How can your testimony help another victim?

_____

_____

_____

_____

_____

_____

_____

_____

_____

_____

_____

_____

_____

_____

_____

_____

_____

_____

_____

_____

_____

_____

_____

_____

_____

_____

<u>Prayer</u>: Dear Lord, please forgive those who stole my innocence. Help me to not blame myself for their wrongdoings. Transform my mind so that I may continue to live my life despite the struggles I have endured. In Jesus' name, Amen.

You have just witnessed a series of monologues; a group of individuals who have shared their stories of mental and physical abuse, sexual assault, lies, and the consequences they suffered for taking the wrong choices in life. Many of them also suffered other cruelties inflicted on them by the very people who had the power to help save them.

God works in mysterious ways, and He has anointed me with a gift – to minister their vital messages to you. I pray that you take these messages as a warning, revelation, or a wake-up call in your own life. When you have experienced a wrong turn in life, it will certainly mess you up if you do not consult your heavenly Father. The time has come that you let go and let God have His way. God does not consult the past to determine your future. It is vital that you never place your mouth on people no matter what the situation. Somewhere in your life, you also made a wrong turn and there is some dirt that belongs to YOU! There were times when you use to be really spiritual, but now that Angela /Michael came into your life, you forgot about the Word. You were no longer involved in your church services, you forgot about your love for God and the people who cared about you the most.

God will NOT take a back seat for anyone! God is the giver who granted you the gift that should be a blessing to your spirit. Your life is a gift from God; the way you present it is a gift to God. Do not allow the temptations of the gift to block the blessings of the giver. Once the giver has ordained the gift, embrace it!

People will no longer understand your praise or determination to overcome your sin. Remember your set backs are there to serve as a triumphant come back for where God is going to take you. God is calling you to become a leader to a dying nation. No one said that the road was going to be easy, but continue holding on to God's unchanging Word. Remember, the greatest leader on earth was also a servant. Case in Point, one must serve before they are able to lead. Regardless of the obstacles that you are facing, God has created a way of escape through His Word.

Moreover, we encounter people who go through experiences which are occurring everywhere around us day by day. Often times, these individuals refuse to display their struggles. No matter how close you are to the person, it is your job to allow these individuals to realize that there is a God who sits high and looks low. God has the power to do all things but fail. The wait is OVER and there will be no more delays.

In the book of Ecclesiastes 9:11, Solomon writes, "I returned, and saw under the sun, that the race is not to the swift, nor the battle to the strong, neither yet bread to the wise, nor yet riches to men of understanding, nor yet favour to men of skill; but time and chance happeneth to them all." Race towards your dreams even when you are unable to run. If you are up there in age, begin to walk. If you become too tired to walk, make your way by crawling. If you are too broken to crawl, simply lay down and die for what YOU believe.

The Word of God tells us in James 4:6 (KJV) "But He giveth more grace. Wherefore He saith, God resisteth the proud, but giveth grace unto the humble. Certainly, one must humble themselves and allow God to work according to His plan for their life. When you do not see yourself moving to the next level in God, He may be trying to release you from the last level. Many times, God may have to snatch some things away from you in order for you to gain your authority back. When you are Ordinary, you become perplexed in your arrival to your future. However, when you are Extraordinary, you can lead those who are Ordinary. Being Extraordinary exempts you from the equality of humanity leaving you alienated from the things of this world. Your weakness should never be an excuse for not achieving your fullest potential. Remember, when all else fails, Try God!

ABOUT THE AUTHOR

"Excellence is my purpose; failure is not an option. I strive to be the best because excellence is my purpose."

This quote is from a woman who inspires everyone to always reach for the best in life, Lakisha M. Sanders. She is a native of Albany, Georgia but currently residing in Fort Lauderdale, Florida. Sanders is the epitome of a phenomenal woman. She holds a Master's in Education and is currently working toward her Doctorate, also in Education. She is an actress, designer and playwright. Sanders is a beacon of hope and a magnet for the brokenhearted. She is never too busy to lend a listening ear for those in need and it is inherent in her character to give. Sanders adamantly believes she will reap everything she has sown. Without question, she is a woman of virtue, dignity, and class. She has written her first book, "The Secret Is Out: It's Time To Break Ground" and her desire is to continue writing and taking her career to the next plateau in Jesus Christ.